The Land of
IF ONLY

written by Kelly Swanson

illustrated by Karen C. Eddington

ISBN: 978-0-9816162-2-3

A little story

For those who are small

With a message

Big enough for us all

This book is dedicated to Amanda Marie Swanson
who now dances with angels.

If you had wings
And could fly through the night
Up past the moon
And three stars to the right

If all were clear
Look down and you'd see
The Land of If Only
Come, go there with me

In the Land of If Only
Grass is green, just like ours
Some days bring sun
And others bring showers

There are some who are short
And some who are tall
Some who have much
And some nothing at all

Look in that window
It's baker man Jake
Pounding the dough
For the bread that he makes

See how he's frowning
And shaking his head
He's never quite happy enough
With his bread

It's too thick, it's too light
It's too heavy, he'd say
If only the dough
Would rise faster today

If only I could work
One hour more
I could sell twice as much
Bread as before

Listen, can you hear
Clara May singing?
So clear and so bright
It's like silver bells ringing

But sadly most days
You don't hear a thing
Because most of the time
Clara May does not sing

You see, Clara refuses
To sing unless
She knows that her voice
Is the one they call best

If only I'd get solo
In the church choir
If only I could sing
One octave higher

If only, if only
If only could be
If only, if only
Then happy I'd be

There's Farmer Brown
Pacing this way and that
My pigs are too thin
My horses too fat

You know I've never
Been one to complain
But if only my fields
Got a little more rain

There's Mr. Mailman
Singing the blues
If only I had me
A new pair of shoes

There sits a boy
Who wants to be taller
Next door to a woman
Who wants to be smaller

And there sits poor
Little Sara McGoo
Still watching and waiting
For her dream to come true

If that one were thin
If this one not so poor
If only her wallet
Had one dollar more

If only, if only
It's quite clear to see
How the Land of If Only's
Name came to be

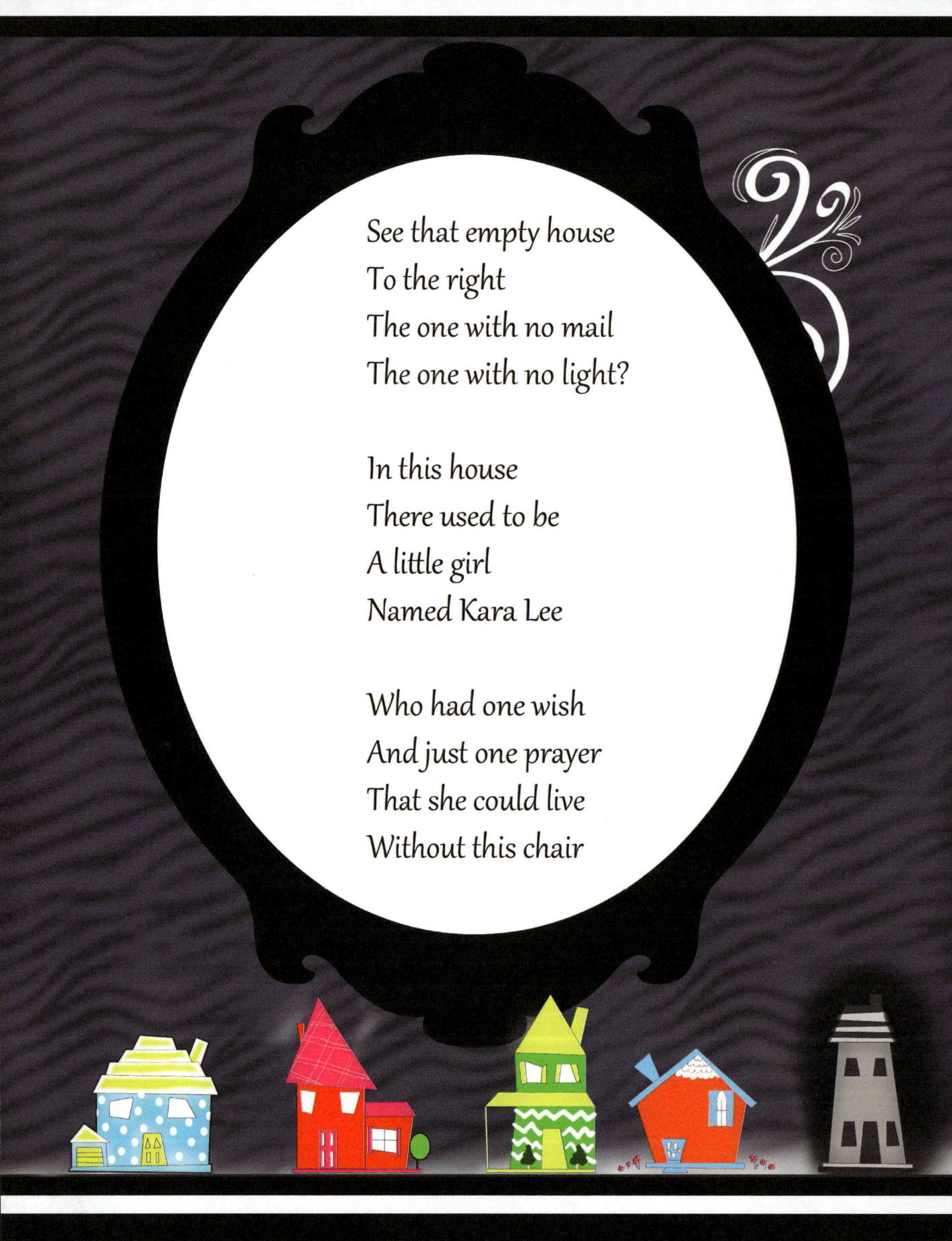

See that empty house
To the right
The one with no mail
The one with no light?

In this house
There used to be
A little girl
Named Kara Lee

Who had one wish
And just one prayer
That she could live
Without this chair

That she'd be given
Just one chance
To spread her arms
Like wings and dance

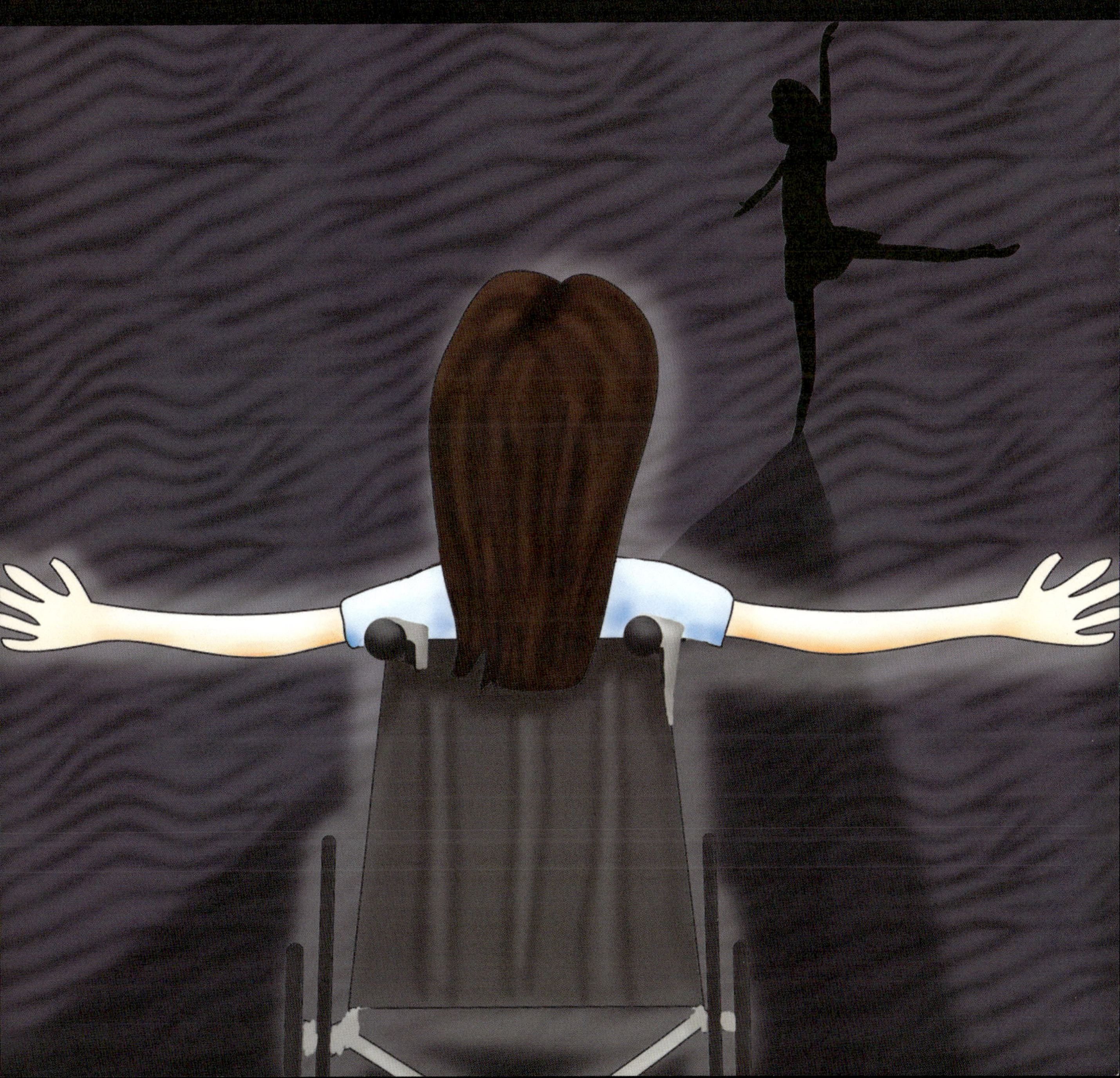

And so she wished
And so she prayed
Whispering If only
She lived her days

And like her neighbors
And neighbors beside her
She lived a life
That couldn't satisfy her

And then one day
There came a girl
With perfect legs
And a golden curl

Who whispered, Come
And go with me
To the place where If Only's
Go to be free

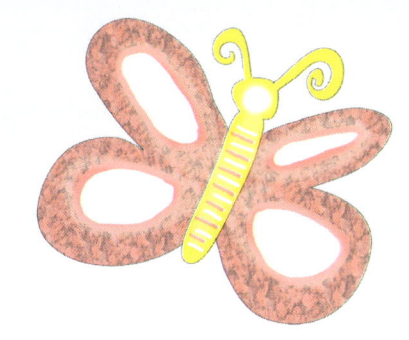

And together they went
Hand in hand
Up over the hill
To the neighboring land

Where the grass is green
Just like ours
Where some days bring sun
And others bring showers

Where some people are short
And some are tall
Some who have much
And some nothing at all

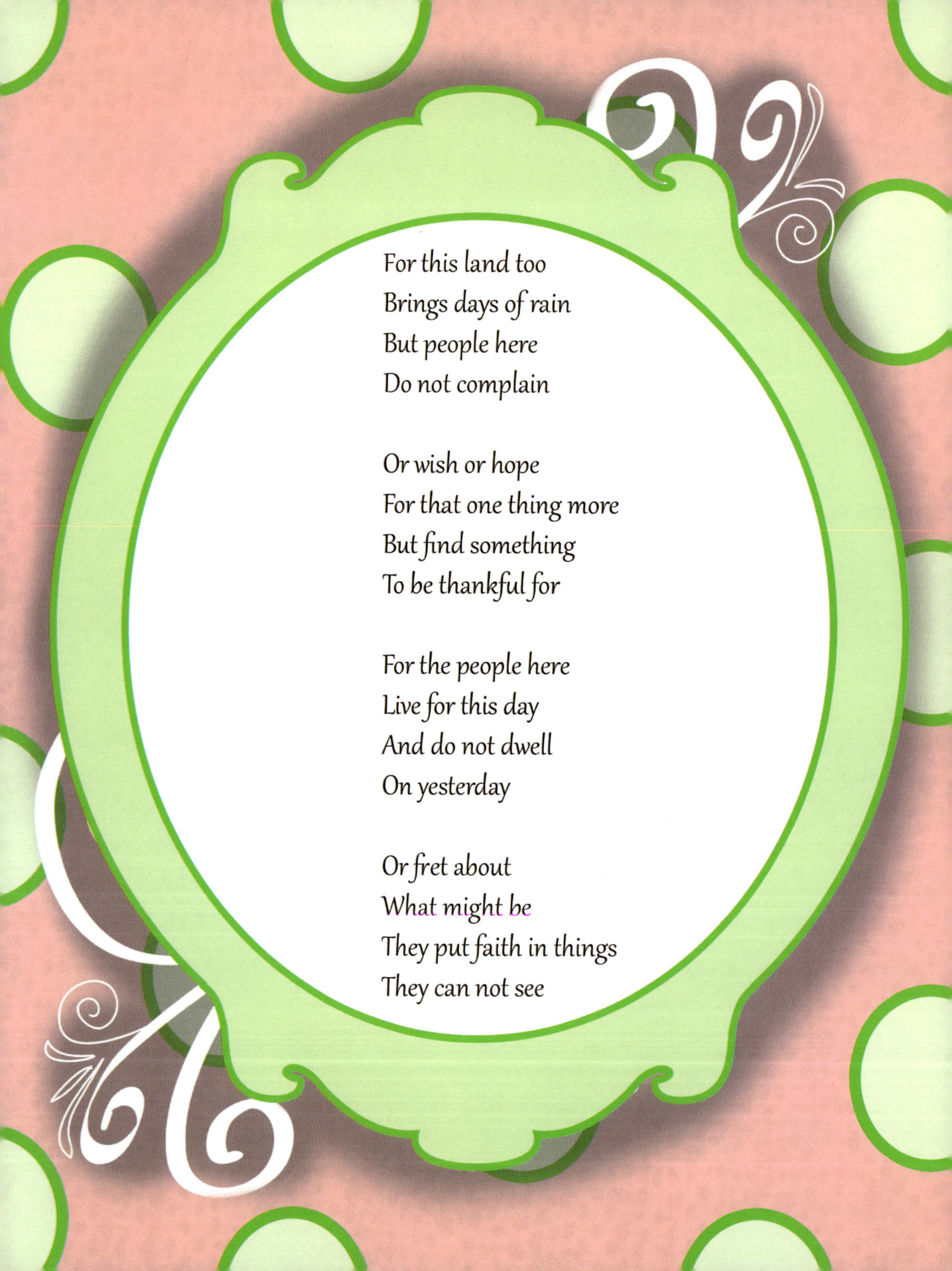

For this land too
Brings days of rain
But people here
Do not complain

Or wish or hope
For that one thing more
But find something
To be thankful for

For the people here
Live for this day
And do not dwell
On yesterday

Or fret about
What might be
They put faith in things
They can not see

For though there's not much
That they can do
To change the road
They can change the view

Beautiful day - the sun is warm - smells like spring

And so they live
Simple and free
Not burdened down
By what could be

And that's when
Little Kara Lee
Gripping her chair whispered
What about me?

And so answered
The little girl
With the perfect legs
And the golden curl

To live here
You must learn to let go
Of all the If Only's
That burden you so

To never wish
For what you have not
To learn to be happy
For the life you've got

Every day you must
Make a choice
To put a smile on your face
And joy in your voice

Find a way to fill your day
With laughter
And you can stay here
In Happily Ever After

It's a beautiful life

Good friends

I'm thankful to be me

I can see   smell   feel

Family

And a smile broke out
On Kara's face
For hope at last
Had found a place

And she closed her eyes
Counted to three
Took all those If Only's
And set them free

And there she lived
And there she stayed
And still she dreamed
And still she prayed

And let go of that
Not meant to be
And at last she lived
Most happily

And that's why in If Only
That last house to the right
There sits no mail
And there is no light

We hear someone new
Is about to move in
And, alas, the story
Starts over again

In Happily Ever After
Kara Lee stayed
Until the stars came
To take her away

And now you'll find
On the very best night
When the moon is full
And the stars are bright

If you look way up
Into the sky
You can see Kara Lee
Spread her wings - And fly

For at last
And not by chance
She finally got her wish
...To dance

Are you living in the land of If Only?

If you live burdened
By what could be
And need something
To set you free

If this is you
Then so I pray
That you would hear me
When I say

Close your eyes
Count to three
Take your If Only's
And set them free

For what will come
Will come despite
Your greatest effort
And your greatest might

And though you can't always
Stop the storm
Or change the road
On which you were born

When you've done all
You know to do
You still have the power
To change your view

Please know you always
Have a choice
To smile through the pain
And put joy in your voice

So in this day may
You choose laughter
And join me in the land

Of Happily-Ever-After

Acknowledgements

I hope you enjoyed this simple story, and that its message landed in your heart at a time when you really needed to hear it. Life doesn't promise you a happily ever after. We aren't guaranteed that all we hope to pass will come to pass. We live in a society that teaches us happiness will come once we achieve, attain, or access something over the rainbow – that something just outside our reach. And so we wait for love, money, power, things, beauty, or status to complete us. The truly lucky ones learn that contentment is something we choose in the here and now – while we reach over the rainbow – the peace we hold in the middle of the rain.

So, while the fairy tale isn't real, and life doesn't come with a happily-ever-after guarantee – I know something that does. I know a true Prince and a loving King. And I stand on His promise that there is something better out there waiting for me. I couldn't let you close this book without telling you about the happily-ever-after that I know without a doubt is waiting for me – in brilliant full-fledged color – the one that has been promised to me and paid for by the blood of Jesus Christ – the one who will wipe away every tear, and make every body new.

Accepting Him as my Lord and savior was the single most important decision I ever made and I have not for one single moment regretted it. And now I walk in peace, faith, and confidence – knowing what is waiting for me – and the power that fills me even now as I walk this earth. I know what it feels like to look to the world to fill that empty place, only to find that the empty place was created for only Him to fill. And without Him, you will never know true peace. You can discount this as the ramblings of a fool (you wouldn't be the first) or you can listen close knowing this will be the most important information you will ever receive. And you will feel the love and grace in which I have wrapped it. For it truly is a gift. Not from me. From Him. And He wants you to open it.

So you can call me the author of this story, but I would be remiss if I didn't give credit where credit is due. The true message was not from me – but from your heavenly Father – who sees you sitting there in the dark – who knows your pain – and who in this moment used me and allowed me this opportunity to explain to you the hope that is within me. And the hope that waits for you. If you already know Him, then be reminded of what you have, and the inheritance to which you have already begun receiving. And turn your eyes back to Him – your healer and your redeemer.

If you don't know Him – this Jesus of whom I speak – or if perhaps what you know is misguided – then please give Him another chance. Seek Him. Knock and He will answer. He's right here with His hand outstretched. And if I can help you get to know Him better, just call me or email me and I will share what He has done in my life. It would be my greatest honor. Thank you for letting me have this moment.

Love your wacky motivational speaker who found something so much better than a fairy godmother,

Kelly Swanson

For God so loved the world that he gave his one and only Son,
that whoever believes in him shall not perish but have eternal life.
John 3:16